Making Love Last a Lifetime

BIBLICAL PERSPECTIVES ON LOVE, MARRIAGE, AND SEX

PASTOR'S GUIDE

by Martha Ann Pilcher

ABINGDON PRESS
Nashville

Making Love Last a Lifetime:
Biblical Perspectives on Love, Marriage, and Sex

Pastor's Guide

Copyright © 2004 by Abingdon Press.

All rights reserved. No part of this work may be reproduced or transmitted in any form or by any means, electronic or mechanical, including photocopying and recording, or by any information storage or retrieval system, except as may be expressly permitted by the 1976 Copyright Act or in writing from the publisher. Requests for permission should be addressed in writing to Permissions Office, 201 Eighth Avenue, South, P.O. Box 801, Nashville, Tennessee 37202-0801, faxed to 615-749-6512, or e-mailed to permissions@abingdonpress.com.

Scripture quotations in this publication, unless otherwise indicated, are from the New Revised Standard Version of the Bible, copyrighted © 1989 by the Division of Christian Education of the National Council of the Churches of Christ in the United States of America, and are used by permission.

This book is printed on acid-free, elemental chlorine-free paper.

ISBN 0-687-74001-0

05 06 07 08 09 10 11 12 13—10 9 8 7 6 5 4 3
Manufactured in the United States of America.

Contents

Introduction
Fishing Expeditions 5
Using This Guide 6

Planning the Program
Gathering Support 7
Tailoring the Program to Your Congregation 7
Setting Up Study Groups 8
Planning Sermons 9
Using the Survey 9
Designing a Kickoff Event 10
Welcoming Visitors 10
Planning Worship 11

Promoting the Program
Announcing From the Pulpit 12
Designing a Promotion Plan 12
Using the Logo 13
Creating Banners, Postcards, Posters, and Flyers 13
Communicating With Your Congregation 13
Communicating With Your Community 14

Analyzing Demographics 15
Finding Media Outlets 15
Creating a Calendar 15

Evaluating the Program
Using Evaluation Tools 16

CD-ROM Contents

Planning the Program
Adam Hamilton Video Excerpt
Script to Introduce the Program
PowerPoint Presentation
Congregational Survey
Sermon Starters
Scripture References
Ideas for Children's and Youth Programs
Calendar

Promoting the Program
Promotion Plan
Logo
Banner
Postcard Copy
Poster/Flyer
Articles for Church Newsletter
Press Releases
Advertising Copy
Public Service Announcement Copy

Evaluating the Program
Congregational Evaluation Form
Leader/Teacher Evaluation Form
Planning Team Evaluation Form

INTRODUCTION

Making Love Last a Lifetime: Biblical Perspectives on Love, Marriage, and Sex is a small-group study that is more than a small-group study. It provides the components to create a powerful small-group experience, including video presentations; a leader's guide with activities for class sessions and home use; and a thoughtful, inspiring participant's book written by Adam Hamilton, the dynamic young pastor of the United Methodist Church of the Resurrection in Leawood, Kansas.

But it is more than that. This pastor's guide with CD-ROM gives you the information and tools needed to create a congregationwide event that will reach beyond the classroom, beyond the sanctuary, and into the community, bringing young people and families into your church.

Making Love Last a Lifetime is a comprehensive program for reaching new people, creating excitement, launching new small groups, and strengthening existing classes. It includes sermon starters, marketing materials, and outreach tools, built around an eight-week study on a topic that holds great interest for singles and for married persons, both inside and outside the church.

Fishing Expeditions

At a Christmas candle-lighting service three years ago, Adam Hamilton announced that beginning in January, he would be preaching a series of sermons on love, marriage, and sex. The sanctuary was packed with visitors at that candle-lighting service, and many of them returned in January to hear what this dynamic young pastor had to say on a topic that was of vital interest to them. So many returned, in fact, that during the usually slow months of January and February, worship attendance actually increased between twenty and fifty percent, depending on the Sunday, over attendance in December! Overall attendance was up over thirty percent.

Making Love Last a Lifetime is based on that sermon series. Like the series, it is what Adam Hamilton calls a "fishing expedition," drawing from Jesus' invitation to the first disciples to become "fishers of people." Details of Hamilton's experience, as well as his descriptions of other fishing expeditions, can be found in his book *Unleashing the Word,* published by Abingdon Press.

We encourage you to make use of this pastor's guide to create a fishing expedition of your own, inviting people into the church and then following through with sermons, worship activities, and the video-based small-group study that is the core of this program.

Using This Guide

How can you have a successful fishing expedition? This pastor's guide and the accompanying CD-ROM will help you take the video-based study and turn it into an eight-week, churchwide event that can include:

- Announcement from the pulpit at a high-attendance worship service
- Congregational survey on attitudes about love, marriage, and sex
- Sermons using sermon starters and survey results
- Multiple small-group studies, with existing and new small groups
- Coordination with youth, children's, and family programs
- Promotion and publicity in your surrounding community

Take a few minutes and look through this pastor's guide and CD-ROM. Throughout this guide, whenever one of the CD-ROM components is mentioned, it will be printed in **bold** with this symbol ⊕ shown in the margin.

Planning the Program

Gathering Support

An important first step is gathering support for the program. Set up a meeting with your key members, staff, and education leaders. Show an excerpt from the videos. **(See CD-ROM: Adam Hamilton Video Excerpt.)** Introduce them to this study. **(See CD-ROM: Script to Introduce the Program and PowerPoint Presentation.)** Enlist their support in the project, and get whatever approvals are needed. At this meeting, create a planning team to set up and coordinate the program.

Gather the support of current Sunday school teachers and other workers with children, youth, and adults. Encourage all of them to participate in the study to help it become a churchwide event. Recruit adult leaders to facilitate new small groups that may be organized for the event, to accommodate existing members, new members, and visitors.

As you recruit and gather support, emphasize that *this study has the potential to increase dramatically the number of participants in your small groups.*

Tailoring the Program to Your Congregation

The planning team's first job is to decide which parts of the program your church will use. Look at the components included in *Making Love Last a Lifetime* and tailor it to your congregation.

Along with your education leaders, review the video-based small-group study that forms the basis of the program. Components of the study include:

- a DVD and videocassette containing eight fifteen-minute presentations, one for each of the eight class sessions
- a leader's guide with discussion questions and activities, suggestions for facilitating class sessions, and reproducible activity pages for use by participants
- Adam Hamilton's book *Making Love Last a Lifetime: Biblical Perspectives on Love, Marriage, and Sex*

Decide which elements of the program you will use in addition to the small-group study. Here are some of your options; you may think of more.

- Worship and sermons coordinated with small-group study topics **(See CD-ROM: Sermon Starters.)**
- Congregational survey to gather information for sermons **(See CD-ROM: Congregational Survey.)**
- Coordinated youth and children's activities **(See CD-ROM: Ideas for Children's and Youth Programs.)**
- Promotional activities in the church and community **(See CD-ROM: Promoting the Program.)**

Setting Up Study Groups

Determine the number of small groups that will participate in the study and when they will meet. Existing classes may decide to use the study, especially couples groups. You may also want to organize new classes especially for this event, meeting Sunday morning or during the week. At Church of the Resurrection, small groups launched during studies like this one have become an ongoing and central part of the church's ministry.

Be sure to offer a variety of meeting times—on Sunday mornings and during the week—to accommodate the busy schedules of members and visitors from the community.

Planning Sermons

If you decide to create a "fishing expedition" around this program, one of the key elements will be sermons. Ideally, the topics you cover in your weekly sermons will correspond in some way with the small-group study topics. That way, people throughout the congregation will have concepts and issues reinforced each week in a variety of settings.

The intent is not to have you repeat the points made by Adam Hamilton in his book and video presentations; rather, you should present your own ideas on these topics. To help you with that process, we have provided the Scripture references used each week in the study **(See CD-ROM: Scripture References.)** and sermon starters to stimulate your thinking about the topics. **(See CD-ROM: Sermon Starters.)** As part of your sermons or worship services, you may want to have couples from your congregation share briefly some of their own experiences, either in person or on video.

Using the Survey

In the videos for the small-group study, you will hear Adam Hamilton refer to a survey on love, marriage, and sex that he conducted at his church. In the videos he uses the results of the survey to dramatic and humorous effect.

On the CD-ROM included with this guide, we have provided Adam Hamilton's survey, which we encourage you to use with your own congregation. **(See CD-ROM: Congregational Survey.)** Individual responses will be confidential, of course; but the statistics and anonymous comments can be tabulated and used in your sermons to ensure that your remarks really reflect the needs and concerns of your particular community.

Be sure to distribute the survey well in advance of the event itself, for sermon planning purposes but also because it serves as an effective announcement of the upcoming series.

At Church of the Resurrection, the surveys were handed out with the bulletins by the ushers at the beginning of the service. Pencils were in the seatbacks throughout the sanctuary. Adam Hamilton took eight minutes near the beginning of the worship service to ask the congregation to fill out these surveys and return them. He walked the congregation through the survey, pointing out which section was to be filled out by whom, and then asked for the congregation's assistance. If you follow a similar procedure, not everyone will return a survey; but you will be surprised by the large number of persons who will. You will likely continue to receive these surveys in the mail during the following week, as some people will choose not to fill them out in the presence of their mates.

Designing a Kickoff Event

Your kickoff event can consist of whatever you think works best for your congregation: a weekend of activities, a special evening event, a worship service, a luncheon after worship. The timing should coincide with the date of the first sermon being preached. (If sermons are not used, a kickoff event of this type may not be helpful.)

Here are some ideas you might use:

- Show sample video clips from the study.
- Introduce the leaders of the small-group studies.
- Preview some of the survey results.
- Ask one or more couples to describe what makes their marriages strong and to stress the need for this study.
- Offer a display of resources.
- Pass out sign-up forms for study groups.
- Provide lots of food!

Welcoming Visitors

In the long run, the success of this program in bringing in new members will depend on how visitors are treated when they arrive. It is helpful, during this program or anytime, to post "welcomers" at key entry points in your building; but ultimately the welcome that visitors feel will depend on the actions of all church members.

Planning the Program

- Remind members of the importance of welcoming visitors.
- Make announcements about this in worship services and Sunday school classes.
- Put notices in the church newsletter.
- Put up posters around the building.

Be sure to follow up on every first-time visitor who attends a worship service or participates in a small group during this program. For a detailed description of how Church of the Resurrection does this, see Adam Hamilton's book *Leading Beyond the Walls* and its chapter on "Effective Follow-up."

Planning Worship

Worship services will play a key role in the success of this study series because more people will be reached at these services than at any other time. In addition to the sermon, there are other aspects of the service that can be tailored to the program:

- Use appropriate Scripture. **(See CD-ROM: Scripture References.)**
- Choose hymns and anthems to accompany the theme.
- Provide handouts in the pews or bulletins, including information about how to sign up for study groups.
- Ask married couples to serve as ushers.
- Ask married couples to speak about the importance of their faith to their marriage.
- Provide evaluation forms for the last service of the series (See below: Evaluating the Program.).

Promoting the Program

Announcing From the Pulpit

Adam Hamilton found that at Church of the Resurrection, the most effective way to promote and publicize the program was to announce it from the pulpit at the worship service most likely to attract visitors from the community. At his church, that was the Christmas candle-lighting service; for yours it might be Easter or some other traditional Christmas service.

People from the community do attend your church; they just do not come often enough. Catch them when you have them, and offer a warm invitation to return. Be "fishers of people," using important, high-profile topics that members of your community find compelling, such as love, marriage, and sex.

Along with the announcement, be sure to distribute copies of the congregational survey; and consider providing time during or after the service for people to fill it out. **(See CD-ROM: Congregational Survey.)**

Designing a Promotion Plan

Find someone who is a good communicator to help here. If you have members of the congregation with experience in public relations or marketing, recruit them to help. Work together to create a promotion plan. **(See CD-ROM: Promotion Plan.)**

Using the Logo

Every successful project has a logo that gives it a visual identity. Think about Coca-Cola, Nike, and businesses in your area that you recognize as soon as you see their logo or colors. That is what you want to aim for: immediate visual recognition. You can use the logo provided or develop one of your own. **(See CD-ROM: Logo.)** Once you select a logo, use it everywhere!

Creating Banners, Postcards, Posters, and Flyers

You will need some materials to help you spread the word about your program. One simple, effective way to do this is to hang a banner outside your church, so that people in the community and those driving by can learn about the program and be invited to attend. **(See CD-ROM: Banner.)**

Postcards have multiple uses: in mailings to your members and community, in pew racks for pickup during worship, as follow-up for visitors on Monday mornings. One of the best uses is giving them to members to hand out to friends. **(See CD-ROM: Postcard Copy.)**

Develop your own poster, or use the one provided. When duplicated at 8½ x 11 inches, it can serve as a flyer; when enlarged on a photocopier, it can be posted around the building. **(See CD-ROM: Poster/Flyer.)**

Communicating With Your Congregation

Do not forget the importance of making your own congregation aware of what is happening.

- Announce the upcoming program in worship services, bulletins, and newsletters.
- If you decide to use the congregational survey, hand out copies of the survey during or after worship services, in adult Sunday school classes, and at weekday programs.
- After the initial announcement or kickoff, include regular

- reminders in the church bulletin or newsletter. **(See CD-ROM: Articles for Church Newsletter.)**
- Put handouts or postcards in the pews and several high-traffic areas of the church.
- Hang posters around the building.
- Create a bulletin board, using the logo, posters, and other information provided.
- If your church has a website, use it to promote the program.
- In worship services leading up to the program, ask married couples to take a few minutes to talk about their marriages and the importance the church has played in them.

Communicating With Your Community

Some of the best ways to spread the word in your community are low-cost and low-tech. Hang a banner outside your church, as described above. Display posters or flyers at community centers, grocery stores, hardware stores, beauty salons, barbershops, and other high-traffic areas. Mail or hand out postcards in the community. Probably the best method of all is to have church members invite their friends and neighbors to attend the study. Give them copies of the postcard or flyer to use.

We live in an age of mass media. For churches that choose to, using the media to spread your message can be effective; and, if done wisely, it can also be inexpensive.

How do you decide where to put your efforts? Conduct an informal survey of members and ask them what newspapers they read, radio stations they listen to, television stations they watch, and other sources of information they rely upon. Use the results in developing your marketing plan.

We have included in the program several items that you can use or adapt for use with the media. These are:

- Press releases for local newspapers **(See CD-ROM: Press Releases.)**
- Advertising copy for use in developing newspaper ads **(See CD-ROM: Advertising Copy.)**
- Public service announcements for radio and television (A public

service announcement, or PSA, is a free "ad" that broadcast outlets are required to use. Keep in mind, however, that they receive numerous PSAs and cannot use all of them.) **(See CD-ROM: Public Service Announcement Copy.)**

Analyzing Demographics

Demographics are the statistical characteristics or profiles of groups. As you plan your media activities, think about the types of people you are trying to reach with your message. Then contact the newspapers, radio stations, and television stations to get their demographics.

As a general rule, newspapers are effective in reaching people over thirty; and television is good for reaching people in their twenties. However, there are always exceptions to the rule, such as special newsletters or local radio and television talk shows.

Finding Media Outlets

Send out news releases four weeks prior to your program, and give them to both the religion and lifestyles editors of the newspapers. Send out public service announcements two weeks in advance to the radio stations and to the community relations people at the local television stations.

If there are any locally produced talk shows on area radio or television stations, call the stations and talk with the producers. Let them know about your church's program, and offer to have someone come and talk about it on the air. Of course, be sure that the people you send present themselves well, both verbally and visually.

Creating a Calendar

A calendar with event dates and deadlines for projects can be very helpful to everyone involved. First decide on the beginning date for the events; then work backward to tasks that require lead time, such as sending out postcards and organizing media coverage. **(See CD-ROM: Calendar.)**

Evaluating the Program

Evaluation is an important part of any church program—to determine what worked, what did not, and what can be improved next time. Evaluation is especially important with programs such as this one, which may be different from what you have tried before.

Using Evaluation Tools

At the end of the study series, get your planning team back together to discuss strengths and weaknesses of the program. We have provided some tools that may be helpful in this effort.

- At the last worship service of the series, pass out evaluation forms and invite people to help in the evaluation process. **(See CD-ROM: Congregational Evaluation Form.)**
- Give evaluation forms to leaders of all the study groups. **(See CD-ROM: Leader/Teacher Evaluation Form.)**
- Analyze attendance numbers and other pertinent information. Were new groups formed? How many visitors and new members were there? Was attendance consistent throughout the series? Would you consider it a success? **(See CD-ROM: Planning Team Evaluation Form.)**
- Look at options for future study series. Check AbingdonPress.com and Abingdon Press catalogs for other video-based series, such as *Beginnings: An Introduction to Christian Faith* and *Sisters: Bible Study for Women.*